About the Author

Nick Jacobson was born in the Bay Area, California, on 18 April 1990. He has one sister and two loving parents. He was raised right but got caught up in the life of the streets at a young age. He started off on the journey of life in the wrong direction, where he made lots of mistakes. He was a young teen when he first got incarcerated and ended up in the juvenile hall.

Now he is currently working on becoming a better man with principles and morals. He is the founder of a non-profit organization called "Keep Us Healthy". His non-profit organization's main focus is about reforming the healthcare system behind the walls.

He believes in God, family and being successful. He is ambitious and focused on goals. Something that helped him with this recipe book is his love of food and that he went to Le Cordon Bleu in San Francisco, where he graduated in 2010.

He is currently incarcerated in a California State Prison, where he is working toward earning his freedom.

SPREAD: 30

Nick Jacobson

SPREAD: 30

Olympia Publishers
London

www.olympiapublishers.com
OLYMPIA PAPERBACK EDITION

Copyright © Nick Jacobson 2024
Illustrations by A. Jacobson

The right of Nick Jacobson to be identified as author of
this work has been asserted in accordance with sections 77 and 78 of
the Copyright, Designs and Patents Act 1988.

All Rights Reserved

No reproduction, copy or transmission of this publication
may be made without written permission.
No paragraph of this publication may be reproduced,
copied or transmitted save with the written permission of the publisher,
or in accordance with the provisions
of the Copyright Act 1956 (as amended).

Any person who commits any unauthorized act in relation to
this publication may be liable to criminal
prosecution and civil claims for damage.

A CIP catalogue record for this title is
available from the British Library.

ISBN: 978-1-80074-929-0

This is a work of fiction.
Names, characters, places and incidents originate from the writer's
imagination. Any resemblance to actual persons, living or dead, is
purely coincidental.

First Published in 2024

Olympia Publishers
Tallis House
2 Tallis Street
London
EC4Y 0AB

Printed in Great Britain

Dedication

I'd like to dedicate this book to my mom and sister. The two most important women and people in my life.

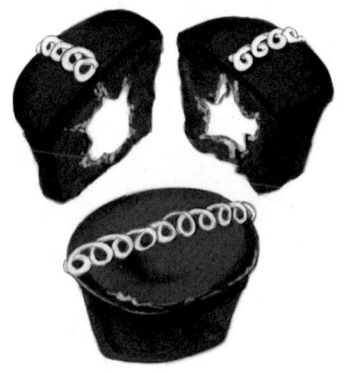

Acknowledgements

I'd like to send a special thanks to my family and loved ones who have held me up in my times of need. The people who struggled with me through my trials and tribulations. Thank you! Most of all, to Brad and Sandi. Andrea Jacobson, thank you for the illustrations. I love you forever! A very special thank you to God for helping me get through the darkness and into the light.

Thank you for purchasing my recipe book, ***SPREAD: 30***.

I have collected a variety of different meals to cook over the years of being incarcerated. They are fun, simple recipes most of the time and tasteful. If you are doing time or even going to college and need to save money for tuition. I hope you can find something in here to accommodate you and make your situation a little easier.

If you have ever done time or are doing time, you know the food provided by your institution is usually not enough. Plus, not to mention disgusting. Most of the time, you get served bologna sandwiches for lunch and a pathetic dinner which usually consists of some type of mystery meat with some fake potatoes and a little bit of vegetables. So, to eat something a little more exciting, we cook spreads.

A basic way to explain a spread is a mix of soups, chips and meat in a bag with a variety of whatever you can think of to make it taste better, like pork rinds, pickles, etc. Use your imagination. Though not all these recipes are technically a spread; they still fall into the same category in my eyes when cooking behind the walls.

I include in the pages to come a handful of spread recipes that also include different nachos, burritos, desserts, candies, drinks: even how to make pruno, which is jailhouse alcohol which you make by fermenting oranges and fruit. The things we learn to make while behind the walls, lol. I also believe cooking while behind the walls is a way to bring people together and brighten up an ugly situation in "the land of the lost".

I believe this book will help people living on a budget, from people going to college or going through the struggle and anyone who loves a variety of foods.

So again, thank you for purchasing my book, and I hope you enjoy it!

Basic Spreads

A Spread is the most commonly eaten meal in jail with many different flavors and tastes that are simple to make. Usually they consist of ramen noodles, chips, meat, pickles, and occasionally beans and rice. Also, veggies if preferred. They are not the healthiest meals and I would not recommend them if you are trying to diet or lose weight. Usually, when you are in jail or prison, inmates depend on commissary to make meals that remind them of the outside world. Typical meals served to inmates consist of "mystery meat", soy meat, and other disgusting meals that aren't the least bit filling and, honestly, they are depressing. Spreads bring people together and make time easier in jail or prison. Also, if you are on a budget in the real world, they could help you save money and make quick simple meals – Perfect for college students.

Contents

Basic Spreads 13
Cheezy Bean Spread 19
Tang Spread 20
Cheese & A Pickle Spread 21
Sweet & Sour Spread 22
Orange Chicken Spread 23
Cheesy Chicken & Rice Spread 24
Cheesy Corn Chip Spread 25
Poetry Therapy 26
Cheesy Chicken Ranch Sandwich 27
Philly Cheese Steak 28
BBQ Pulled Beef Sandwich 29
Chili Cheese Frito Bowls 30
Stuffed Crust Pizza 31
MacJackson-ritto 32
Gumbo 33
Tuna casserole 34
Cheesy Rice Layered Pour Over 35
Tuna Rice Plate 36
Self-Worth 37
Cup Burrito 38
Giant Tamale 40
Tamale Pie 42
Posole 44
Nachos 46
Tamale 48
Chicken Cheese Quesadilla 50
Armlength Burrito 51
Get Educated 53
Fillmoe Rice Bowl 54

Chow Mein 56
Teriyaki Chicken 58
Dub's Szechuan 59
Panda Delight 60
Sweet & Sour Pour Over 61
Advice 62
Sunday Brunch 63
Breakfast Burrito 64
Candied Oatmeal 66
Breakfast Cakes 67
Time to Shine 68
Honey Bun Delight 69
Sweet Popcorn 70
Banana Pudding 71
Caramel Apple Lollipops 73
Banana Cream Chocolate Cake 74
Lollipops 76
Chocolate Covered Honey Buns w/Reese's 77
Chocolate Covered Twinkies 78
Banana Crumble Cake Pudding 79
Boyca's Chocolate Cake 80
Cycles of Life 82
Orange Passion 83
Jail House Horchata 85
Cadillac Coffee 86

Cheezy Bean Spread

Ingredients:

3 Top Ramen Soups
1 Bag of Refried Beans
4 Cheese Slices
Cheese Puffs
5oz Meat Log
Pork Cracklins or Jalapeno Pretzels
2 Cups Water
Plastic Bread Bag

Directions:

1. Add Top Ramen with 2 Top Ramen seasonings & Refried Beans in bag with hot water & cook.
2. Smash up Cheese Puffs & Cheese slices add to bag & mix well.
3. Cut up Meat Log & add with Pork Cracklins or Jalapeno Pretzels into bag & mix well.
4. Serve and enjoy.

Tang Spread

Ingredients:

3 Top Ramen Soups
6oz Packet of Orange Kool-Aid
5oz Meat Log
Pork Cracklins or Jalapeno Pretzels
1 ½ Cup Water
Plastic Bread Bag
Handful Cheese Puffs

Directions:

1. Cook Top Ramen with boiling water in bag.
2. Add 1 seasoning packet and 4 oz of orange Kool-aid. Mix well.
3. Add handful of Cheese Puffs & break up to dust.
4. Add cooked Meat Log & Pork Cracklins or Jalapeno Pretzels.
5. Mix ingredients well.
    Serve & enjoy!

Cheese & A Pickle Spread

Ingredients:

3 Top Ramen Soup
1 Bag of Cheese Puffs
4 Cheese Slices
5 oz Meat Log
1 Pickle
Pork Cracklins or Jalapeno Pretzels
1 ½ Cup water
Plastic Bread Bag

Directions:

1. Break Top Ramen up in bag with 1 Top Ramen seasoning & cook in hot water. Cook noodles for approximately 4-5 minutes.
2. Mash up Cheese Puffs add with Cheese slices into bag & mix well.
3. Cut Meat Log & pickle into pieces add to bag with Pork Cracklins or Jalapeno Pretzels & mix well.
4. Serve in two portions and enjoy.

Sweet & Sour Spread

Ingredients:

3 Top Ramen Soup
6 oz Fruit Punch or Cherry Kool-Aid
5 oz Meat Log
1 Pickle
Pork Cracklins or Jalapeno Pretzels
1 Handful of Hot Cheese Crunchies
1 ½ Cup Water
Plastic Bread Bag

Directions:

1. Break up Top Ramen Soup in bag and cook with hot water.
2. Add 1 Top Ramen seasoning packet, 4 oz Kool-Aid and hot chips.
3. Cut up Meat Log and add.
4. Add Pickle and Pork Cracklins or Jalapeno Pretzels.
5. Mix well and serve.

Orange Chicken Spread

Ingredients:

2 Top Ramen Packages
2 Spanish Rice
1 Orange Kool-Aid
2 Chicken Pouches
1 Meat Log
1 Pork Cracklin or Jalapeno Pretzels
1 ½ Cup Hot Water
1 Plastic Bag

Directions:

1. Break up Ramen noodles into bag.
2. Add rice & hot water.
3. Once noodles & rice are cooked add Orange Kool-Aid & mix well.
4. Add chicken and meat (optional to cook log first).
5. Add Pork Cracklins. Mix well and serve.

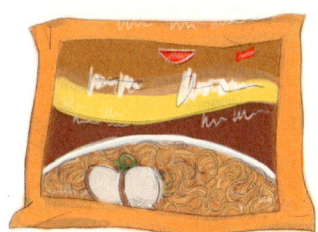

Cheesy Chicken & Rice Spread

Ingredients:

4 Spanish Rice
1–2 Chicken Pouches
Pork Cracklins
4 Cheese Slices
1 Nacho Cheese Dip
1 Cheese Puffs
1 Sliced Jalapeno
1 Plastic Bag

Directions:

1. Cook rice in bag.
2. Cut up Meat Log and cook to preference.
3. Add crumbled cheese slices & cheese dip into rice – mix well.
4. Mix in meat, chips, Pork Cracklins and Jalapeno slices.

*Note: You may need to add a bit more water into spread at Step 4 to ensure the chips do not dry up all the moisture.

Cheesy Corn Chip Spread

Ingredients:

2 Top Ramen Soups
1 Refried Beans
1 Chili Corn Chips
Bag Cheese Puffs or Cheese Crunchies
4 Cheese Slices
1 Pickle
1 Meat Log
Pork Cracklins
1 ½ Cup Hot Water
1 Plastic Bag

Directions:

1. Break up Ramen Noodles into bag. Add beans, hot water & cook.
2. Smash up Chili Corn Chips & Cheese Chips – add to bag. Mix well.
3. Add Cheese slices – Mix well.
4. Chop up Meat Log & slice pickle. Add to bag.
5. Add Pork Cracklins. Mix well & serve.

Poetry Therapy

I write poetry for fun
It helps clear my mind
Cleansing my thoughts
It's a therapeutic time
Just my pencil and pad
What a beautiful way to vent
We all got things we hold inside
Poetry is a way to express ourselves
In a sense it's another way to be free
Freedom, what a beautiful thing
Poetry is like another way for me to fly
My body is trapped in a cage
But through poetry my mind is free
I can go wherever I want
It almost makes me feel like a bird
High in the sky
It's such a beautiful thing
When I'm writing my poetry between the lines.

Cheesy Chicken Ranch Sandwich

Ingredients:

2 Chicken Pouches
4 Cheese Slices
2 Single Ranch Packets
1 Jalapeno
2 Nacho Cheese Squeeze

Directions:

1. Put chicken in a bowl.
2. Mix in sliced Jalapenos.
3. Crumble Cheese Slices into bowl.
4. Squeeze in Ranch packets.
5. Separate into two portions which are in the shape of the bread you're using and heat until cheese is completely melted; about 2 minutes.
6. Heat Cheese Squeezes & squeeze on top of chicken portions.
7. Fill sandwich bread with portions.
8. Serve with favorite chips of choice.

Philly Cheese Steak

Ingredients:

1 Shredded Beef Pouch or "Beef Tip" Drained of Any Gravy
1 Meat Log
Hand Full of Sliced Jalapenos
4 Cheese Slices
2 Single Nacho Cheese Squeeze
2 Sub Sandwich Rolls

Directions:

1. Shred Meat Log into tiny pieces.
2. Crumble cheese slices.
3. Mix both Meat Log & cheese into shredded beef to create cheese steak mixture.
4. Add Jalapenos into cheese steak mixture & mix thoroughly.
5. Split mixture into two sub sandwich sized portions & microwave until cheese is completely melted; about two minutes.
6. Heat nacho cheese & squeeze onto each sandwich roll.
7. Heat bread for ten seconds if desired.
8. Fill roll with the cheese steak mixture on sub rolls.
9. Best served with chips of choice.

BBQ Pulled Beef Sandwich

Ingredients:

1 Shredded Beef
Pork Cracklins
1 Pickle
6 BBQ Sauce Packs
2 Deli Rolls
Mayo
1 Jalapeno Cheese Squeeze

Directions:

1. Drain Shredded Beef and cook.
2. Mix BBQ sauce packet with cooked Shredded Beef well.
3. Spread mayo on bread to taste.
4. Add BBQ Shredded Beef on bread.
5. Slice pickle and add to sandwich.
6. Add Pork Cracklins to sandwich.
7. Add Cheese Squeeze and enjoy.

*Best served with potato chips.

Chili Cheese Frito Bowls

Ingredients:

2 Bags of Chili Cheese Fritos
1 Chili Pouch
1 Cheesy Rice
2 Cheese Squeeze
1 – 3oz Meat Log
1 Sliced Jalapeno Packet (10 slices)

Directions:

1. Cut up Meat Log in bowl.
2. Place a bag of Fritos in two separate bowls.
3. Cook rice, meat & chili separately.
4. Put a cheese squeeze on top of Fritos.
5. Add layer of rice.
6. Then add layer of chili.
7. Add another layer of Cheese Squeeze.
8. Split & top last bag of Fritos between both bowls.
9. Add the rest of the cheese, meat, Jalapeno & enjoy!

Stuffed Crust Pizza

Ingredients:

16 Tortillas
2 Chicken Pouches
3 Cheese Squeezes
4 Slices of Cheese
5 Ketchup Packets
2 Packs of Jalapenos
5oz Meat Logs

Directions:

1. Put 3ft x 3ft plastic bag down on table.
2. Dip tortillas in water – lay one tortilla in the middle & connect the edges together to make a big circle using 8 tortillas which makes the crust.
3. Put Cheese Squeeze on crust covering all of it.
4. Repeat #2 & lay over first crust with cheese in between.
5. Roll edges of pizza crust to make the edge crust thicker like a pizza.
6. Put ketchup on top of pizza.
7. Add cheese slices ripped up.
8. Slice up Meat Log like pepperoni & top pizza.
9. Add chicken & Jalapenos to top off pizza.
10. Put pizza in microwave oven for 3 minutes.
11. Let sit for a couple of minutes & enjoy!

You can always add another topping that you prefer.

MacJackson-ritto

Ingredients:

1.75oz Dorito Nacho Cheese Chips
1.5oz Meat Log
1 Top Ramen Beef Soup
2oz Cheese Squeeze
6 to 8oz Hot Water

Directions:

1. Cut up meat log & cook for 30 seconds in microwave.
2. Break up Doritos & soup then place in Dorito bag.
3. Add meat & cheese & then shake up bag.
4. Add hot water to bag & then roll up bag & let set for 5 to 10 minutes.
5. Take out of bag & enjoy!

*Can use Chili Cheese Fritos or whatever chips you prefer.

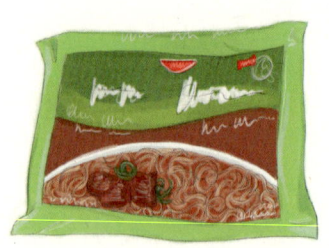

Gumbo

Ingredients:

1 Bag Spanish or White Rice.
1 Slice Jalapeno
1 Can or Pouch of Tuna Fish
1 Pouch of Sardines
1 Meat Log
1 Chicken Pouch
Pork Cracklins as desired
1–2 TSP Siracha or Hot Sauce
1 Chili Soup Seasoning
2 ½ Cups Water
Plastic Bag

Directions:

1. Cook rice.
2. Slice Meat Log & cook.
3. Mix tuna, sardines, chicken, jalapenos, hot sauce & chili seasoning into bowl or crock pot.
4. Add 2 ½ cups water to bowl and heat until water boils.
5. Add in cooked rice, cooked meat log, and bowl mixture into a plastic bag or crockpot and mix thoroughly. The Gumbo should be a thick soup/stew consistency.
6. Serve.

Tuna casserole

Ingredients:

8oz White Rice
1 Pickle
1 Cajun Nut Mix
1 Big Meat Log
4oz Tuna
2 Cheese Squeeze
3 to 4 Cheese Slices
2 Hardboiled Eggs

Directions:

1. Dice up meat, pickle & eggs.
2. Add hot water to rice & cook as instructed.
3. Cook & heat.
4. Once rice is cooked, add Cheese Squeeze & sliced cheese.
5. Add tuna & meat & mix well.
6. Then add pickle, Cajun Nut Mix & eggs, then mix well.
7. Once all is mixed together – separate into two bowls & enjoy!

Cheesy Rice Layered Pour Over

Ingredients:

6oz Cheesy Rice
3oz Meat Log
3.5oz Mackerel
2oz Cajun Nut Mix
2oz Cheesy Squeeze
¼ Dill Pickle or Jalapenos Slices
Squeeze-ums Hot Sauce Packet

Directions:

1. Cut up meat log & pickle or Jalapeno in separate bowls.
2. Cook cheesy rice as instructed on package.
3. Heat meat log & mackerel in microwave for 1 minute.
4. Put rice on plate.
5. Add meat log & mackerel to layer the top of the rice.
6. Sprinkle Cajun nut mix on top of meat.
7. Sprinkle pickle or Jalapeno on top of Cajun nut mix.
8. Put cheese squeeze in bowl & add a little hot water & stir until like consistency of nacho cheese.
9. Pour cheese over all.
10. Add hot sauce & enjoy!

Tuna Rice Plate

Ingredients:

10oz Tuna
½ Dill Pickle
8oz White Rice
4 Hard Boiled Eggs
5 Mayonnaise Packets
2 Mustard Packets

Directions:

1. Chop pickle & eggs into small pieces – put into bowl.
2. Drain tuna & add to eggs & pickles.
3. Add mayonnaise & mustard – mix to make tuna egg salad.
4. Cook rice as directed.
5. Put rice on two separate plates.
6. Spoon tuna egg salad over rice & enjoy!

Self-Worth

You got to know your self-worth
And never sell yourself short
Soak up knowledge and prosper
Nobody said it was going to be easy
Blessings in disguise help us turn wise
Gifted individuals it's time to thrive
Back against the wall we got to stand tall
Achieve our goals and count them as victories
More blessing to add to our inner strength
Virtue, it's a beautiful thing
Hard work and dedication pays off
Rock bottom we all been there
It's time for the come up
Time to hustle
Focus on a legit check to come up
Put ourselves in the best position to win
God is good, God is great
With him anything is possible
Just keep working…
Just keep working!

Cup Burrito

Ingredients:

½ Tsp Mayo
2 Jailhouse Cups
4 Flour Tortillas
Meat of Choice – 5oz Chicken or Meat Log (chopped/shredded)
4.4 to 6.2oz instant Rice (white or Spanish)
4oz Beans
4 Cheese Slices or Nacho Cheese
1 Cup Cheese Chip/Hot Cheetos
Hot Water
1 Bag

Directions:

1. Coat ½ Tsp. Mayo into the inside of 2 Jailhouse cups.
2. Insert 2 flour tortillas inside each cup.
3. Prepare meat of choice – cooked/warmed if possible.
4. Mix rice, beans, cheese chips/Hot Cheetos in bag.
5. Crumble cheese slices or have nacho cheese set aside and ready.
6. Add meat and cheese inside tortilla.
7. Add bag mix to be about ¼ of the burrito size.
8. Add hot water in cup until it reaches the base of your mix.
9. Repeat instructions until burrito is full. Once full, close the top of your burrito and cook for 5 minutes.

Note: Once your burrito is served, feel free to add more cheese, chili beans, hot sauce or any extra toppings. Pork Cracklins are recommended.

Giant Tamale

Ingredients:

1 Corn Bread Piece
4 Bags of Doritos
1 Bag of Cheese Puffs
5oz Meat Log
Pork Cracklins
1 Chicken Pouch
1 Refried Beans
1 Spanish Rice
4 Slices Cheese
2 Cheese Squeezes
2 Cups Hot Water
2 Plastic Bread Bag

Directions:

1. Combine all chips and cornbread into plastic bread bag. Smash up.
2. Add small amounts of water to mixture & mix until it turns into tamale dough.
3. Lay plastic bread bag flat & flatten tamale dough into a rectangle sheet on top of plastic bag.
4. Cook beans & Spanish Rice in separate bowls.
5. Heat meat.
6. Break up cheese slices & put in the middle of tamale dough.
7. Add cooked rice & beans on top of cheese.
8. Add meat & Pork Cracklins – top with Cheese Squeezes.
9. Once ingredients are added proportionately on tamale dough use the second plastic bread bag to roll the tamale.
10. Tie each end of the plastic bag & microwave until steamed.
11. Cut in half & serve.

Tamale Pie

Ingredients:

1 Bag Nacho Cheese Chips
1 Bag Chili Corn Chips
1 Bag Hot Cheese Crunchies
2 pcs of Cornbread
1 Meat Log
1 Chicken Pouch
1 Cheese Squeeze
1 Cheesy Rice
4oz Refried Beans
1 Chili Pouch
6 Slices of Cheese
12 Jalapeno Slices
1 Plate
1 Bread Bag
Bit of Water

Directions:

1. Take Nacho Cheese Chips, Chili Corn Chips & hot chips & smash to dust.
2. Break up corn bread & put in bag with smashed chips.
3. Add water a little bit at a time until mix chips & corn bread to Masa (approximately 8oz).
4. Cook beans & rice as recommended.
5. Cut up Meat Log.
6. Take Massa from bag & put on a plate, then form a pie crust by flattenng middle of plate & making a thick edge around the plate.
7. Add Cheese Squeeze to the pie crust.
8. Add layer of refried beans.
9. Add layer of rice.
10. Add layer of chili.
11. Add meat on top.
12. Then put slices of cheese on top to cover the whole pie.
13. Add Jalapenos to top.
14. Heat in microwave oven for 2 minutes on high.

Then enjoy!

Posole

Preparation for posole soup begins the night before.

Ingredients:

3 Picante Flavored Corn Nuts
8oz White Rice
Chicken Pouch (diced)
3oz Meat Log
2oz Pork Rinds
3 Chili Lime Seasoning Packets
1/4 of 5oz Tapatio Bottle

Directions:

1. Soak corn nuts 24hrs before you plan on making the meal.
2. Cut up Meat Log & put in bowl or bag with Chicken Pouch.
3. Add 18 to 20oz water to 8oz rice bag seal & let cook.
4. Once rice is cooked heat up meat & add it together in bag or big bowl, then add corn nuts.
5. Take the 3chili lime seasoning packets & mix with 3 cups of hot water, stir to add Tapatio, stir again, add to bowl with the rest.
6. Then add Pork rinds & serve!

Enjoy!

Nachos

Ingredients:

Tortilla Chips (or chip of choice)
4 Cheese Slices
3oz Nacho Cheese Dip
4oz Beans
4oz Spanish Rice
Meat of Choice – 5oz Meat Log, Chicken, Roast or Shredded Beef
Jalapeno Slices
Water

Directions:

1. Add the desirable amount of tortilla chips (or chip of choice) on two plates.
2. Mix cheese slices & nacho cheese in bag.
3. Cook beans with water.
4. Cook Spanish Rice in bowl with water.
5. Prepare meat of choice and set aside. Slice Jalapeños as desired.
6. Microwave cheese and stir until a consistent liquid consistency. Add splash of milk if desired.
7. Placed cooked beans, rice, meat, and cheese over tortilla chips.

8. Note: If you have a lot of chips, you may want to only use half, so they are fully flavorful. Or double the ingredients!

Tamale

Ingredients:

Tamale Masa Dough:
Tortilla Chips or 2 Bags of Nacho Doritos
1 Cheese Puff
1 Hot Chip (Hot Cheese Crunchy)
Plastic Bag
Water

Tamale Filling:
Choice of Meat – 5oz Meat Log or Chicken Pouch
12 Jalapenos
4 Slices Cheese
2 Cheesy Rice
1 Chili Pouch
2 Cheese Squeezes

Directions:

1. Crush finely, all chips in plastic bag.
2. Add warm water to the mix until the consistency is a wet pasty dough. *This creates your Tamale masa dough.
3. Flatten out the masa into one big square and cut in half.
4. Add choice of meat, chili, rice, Jalapenos and cheese to the middle of the masa.
5. Fold the masa at each corner to form into Tamale.
6. Microwave for about 2 minutes until Tamale is cooked thoroughly.
7. Serve with rice & beans if desired.

Chicken Cheese Quesadilla

Ingredients:

½ Chili Pouch or 5oz of Chili
1 Cheese Squeeze
4 Slices of Cheese
½ Chicken Pouch or 2.5oz of Chicken 9 Slices of Jalapenos
2 Flour Tortillas

Directions:

1. Mix cheese squeeze with chili.
2. Put one tortilla on a plate.
3. Spread chili cheese mix onto tortilla.
4. Then layer with chicken.
5. Layer slice cheese over all.
6. Lay second tortilla on top of everything.
7. Microwave for 1 minute or until hot & cheese is melted.
8. Enjoy!

Armlength Burrito

Ingredients:

2 Chicken Pouches
5oz Meat Log – Cut up into Small Pieces
4oz Refried Beans
4oz Cheesy Rice
1 Bag of Spicy Hot Cheetos or Spicy Cheese Puffs
12 Slices of Jalapenos
2 Cheese Squeezes
6 Tortillas
1 Plastic Trash Bag Ripped into 2ft x 3ft Piece
5oz Milk

Directions:

1. Cook beans & rice with hot water in bowl.
2. While beans & rice are cooking lay out plastic on table or bed then get a cup of hot water & dip tortillas individually into water & lay out on center of plastic long way 2x3.
3. Once that is done everything else should be ready to fill the burrito.
4. I would layer beans then the rice in the center of the burrito, long way round, then add Meat Log, chicken, jalapenos & cheese.
5. Last but not least add the hot chips or any chips you choose

really; Doritos, Chili Corn chips, etc. You can also add pork rinds if you prefer but it makes it a little harder to roll.
6. Once everything is portioned on the center of tortilla long ways it is time to roll – literally.
7. The first thing you want to do is fold in the ends about 1–2" after that use plastic to roll the burrito slowly for a perfect arm length burrito make sure you keep the ends in & roll until the burrito forms. Once it is rolled in plastic twist ends & tie.
8. Then push the ends in to compact the burrito & make an arm length breakfast burrito.
9. Poke a couple holes in plastic.
10. Then cook in microwave until hot & serve… Enjoy!

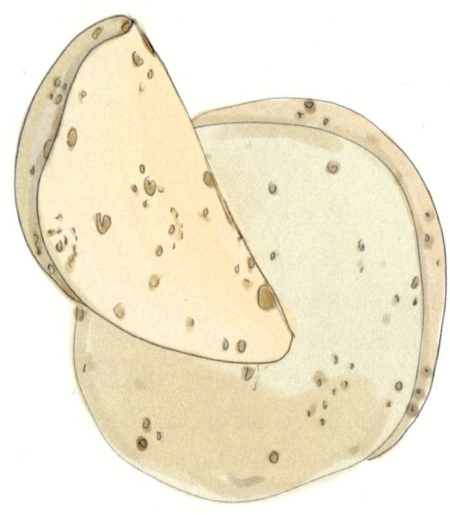

Get Educated

Letting the poetry flow through me
When it comes from the heart
Then you know it's me
The strongest people usually don't have
a choice but to be strong
Trying to right my wrongs and prosper
The mind is a beautiful thing with it you can accomplish your
biggest dreams
Knowledge is power and education is the key to success
In the worst situations remember your blessed
Frustrations messing up your concentration
Misgivings got you down?
Yeah, a quick rebound will have you back in the game
Forget the fame and the limelight
It's time to get educated and your mind right
Hit the books like a crook on a robbery
Yea we need everything!
Philosophy, Real Estate, Stock Exchange
Fuck it politics, economics – We need everything!
Can't forget math got to add it all up!
In the long run we'll watch our bank accounts and add it all up
Motivated and Thankful
Family is everything
God is good, God is great.

Fillmoe Rice Bowl

Ingredients:

5 Jelly Packets
2 Ketchup Packets
2 Mustard Packets
1 Soy Sauce
1 Chicken Pouch
1 – 3oz Meat Log
1 White Rice
1 Cheese Puffs
1 Pork Rinds
1 Flaming Hot Crunchies
1 Beef Seasoning Packet
4 Tsp of Lemonade Kool-Aid
2 Tsp Water

Directions:

1. Combine jelly, ketchup, mustard & soy sauce, beef packets & lemonade blend together.
2. Add 2tsp of water to sauce then stir to nice consistency.
3. Cut up Meat Log & chicken and put into bowl.
4. Add 4tsp of sauce to meat & mix well – then cook for 1 minute.
5. Cook rice as instructed.
6. Turn cheese puffs into dust & then mix with rice in bag.
7. Put Hot Cheetos & pork rinds in bag – add ¾ of sauce in bag & mix well.
8. Put rice into two bowls.
9. Layer meat on top of rice.
10. Layer glazed chips over meat & rice.
11. Take remainder sauce & drizzle over all.
12. Shout out to Fillmoe & Enjoy!

Chow Mein

Ingredients:

Noodles:
3 Instant Ramens – Roast Beef Flavor
2 Mayonnaise Packets
3 Soy Sauce Packets

Topping Ingredients:

1 Pickle with Juice
3oz Meat Log
2oz Pork Rinds
2 – 1oz Jelly Packets
6oz Fruit Punch Kool-Aid

Directions for Noodles:

1. Place noodles in bowl submerge in hot water for 2 minutes then strain water.
2. Then mix in 2 mayonnaise & microwave for 30 seconds in separate bowl.
3. Add soy sauce to mayonnaise.
4. Then add sauce to the noodles & mix together well.
5. Heat up everything together for 4 minutes.

Sauce:

1. Chop up pickle & Meat Log into small pieces.
2. Put inside water pitcher or bowl then add pickle juice, soy sauce, 1 roast beef seasoning packet, 2 jellies & Fruit Punch Kool-Aid.
3. Stir it all together well & then microwave on low for 10 to 15 minutes (check & stir as you go).
4. Once it thickens to a glaze put in big chip bag with pork rinds.
5. Mix well in the chip bag then pour over noodles (or rice if preferred) & enjoy.

*Recommend separating noodles onto two plates then pour sauce equally over both plates if noodles.

Teriyaki Chicken

Ingredients:

8oz White Rice
2 Chicken Pouches
1 Meat Log
1 Bag Pork Cracklins
6oz Ice Tea Kool-Aid
3 to 4oz Soy Sauce

Directions:

1. Add hot water to rice & set aside.
2. Cook chicken & Meat Log together.
3. Pour Ice Tea Kool-Aid into bag or cup; add Soy Sauce. Stir until Kool-Aid is dissolved completely to create Teriyaki Sauce.
4. Heat Teriyaki sauce for about 2 minutes.
5. Once cooked, split rice into 2 bowls or 2 plates. Add chicken, beef & crunched up Pork Cracklins over rice.
6. Add Teriyaki sauce to the amount desired.
7. Enjoy!

Dub's Szechuan

Ingredients:

8oz White Rice
2oz Pork Rinds
8oz Meat Log
1 Bag Cajun Nut Mix
5 Jelly Packets
2 Soy Sauce
2 Syrup Packets
1 to 2 Jalapenos

Instructions:

1. Mix jelly, syrup, soy sauce, Jalapeno & meat log (cut up) in bowl for 5 to 10 minutes.
2. Mix pork rinds & Cajun Nut Mix in bag.
3. Pour sauce with meat into bag & mix until sauce has covered everything.
4. Cook rice with hot water per its directions.
5. Serve rice evenly on two plates.
6. Top rice with mix from bag equally & enjoy!

Panda Delight

Ingredients:

8oz Bag White Rice
8oz Bottle of Jelly
1 Personal Raisin Yogurt Trail Mix Snack
1 Bag Pork Cracklins
4 to 5oz Meat Log or 2oz Meat Log & 2.5oz Chicken Pouch (½ pouch)

Directions:

1. Cook rice as instructed on bag.
2. Cut up meat & mix with pork rinds, trail mix & mix in bowl or microwaveable bag.
3. Cook for 1 ½ minutes then stir or shake bag & then cook for another 1 ½ minutes.
4. Once cooked & stirred thoroughly pour over rice on two separate plates & enjoy!

Sweet & Sour Pour Over

Ingredients:

1 Dill Pickle
1 Fruit Punch Kool-Aid
1 8oz White Rice
1 Pork Rinds
1 5oz Meat Log
1 Hot Cheese Crunchie

Directions:

1. Cut up Meat Log & pickle.
2. Mix Kool-Aid with pickle juice & stir in bowl to make sauce.
3. Cook meat.
4. Smash Hot Cheese Crunchies to dust.
5. Add cooked meat & half the bag of Hot Cheese Crunchies into bowl with sauce then microwave 30 to 45 seconds.
6. Cook rice as instructed on bag & separate on two plates.
7. Put pork rinds in bag with sauce & shake in bag to mix well.
8. Pour over rice & enjoy!

Advice

Everyone needs a helping hand
Life is hard no one said it was easy
Accustomed to a negative life trying to get right
Soul searching trying to find the purpose of life
It's all about your perspective and how you handle situations
God is good, God is great
Every time you fall get back up
Conduct yourself in a professional manner
Strive for perfection
When you're stressed pray and have faith
People come and they go
Real ones will hold you down that's fasho
Positive support system with positive role models
Be a productive person in society
If they on that bullshit cut them off
Leave the past in the past
Focus on success and virtue
Love yourself accordingly
Make your family proud
All that other shit just that other shit
Stick to the plan!

Sunday Brunch

Ingredients:

6 Hardboiled Eggs
4 Triangle Hash Browns (come on S.O.S)
3oz Meat Log
2.5oz Cheesy Rice
4oz Refried Beans
2 Tortillas
1 Syrup Packet
12oz Milk

Directions:

1. Peel eggs & chop up into very small pieces like egg salad put into plastic chip bag or bowl – add 6oz of milk stir & microwave to make scrambled eggs.
2. Cut both Meat Logs in four pieces longways to make small sausage links, soak in syrup & microwave.
3. Cook rice & beans in separate bowls without water.
4. Heat up hash browns until crisp.
5. Once everything is cooked set up on plate in 4 quarter sections of beans, rice, eggs & hash browns then set 4 sausages on top of each & then heat up if needed (I recommend putting some cheese on beans & eggs before you heat it up).
6. Then Serve with tortillas on side plus O.J. or milk – Enjoy!

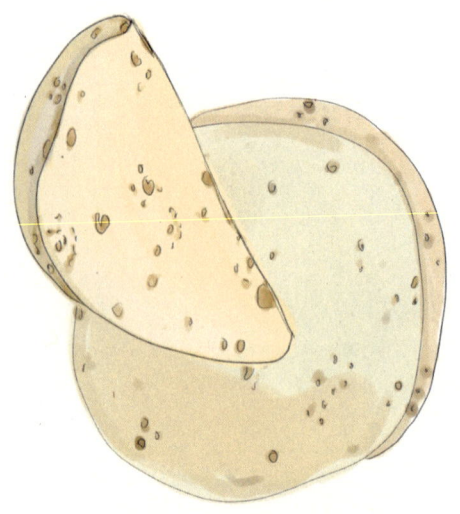

Breakfast Burrito

Ingredients:

5 Hardboiled Eggs – Peeled
5oz Meat Log
4oz Refried Beans
4oz Cheesy Rice
1 Bag of Spicy Hot Cheetos or Spicy Cheese Puffs
12 Slices of Jalapenos
2 Cheese Squeezes
6 Tortillas
1 Plastic Trash Bag Ripped into 2ft x 3ft Piece
5oz Milk

Directions:

1. Peel eggs then chop very small like your making egg salad.
2. Cut up Meat Log & put in bowl or bag with eggs then add milk & cook in microwave.
3. Cook beans & rice with hot water in bowls.
4. While everything is cooking lay out plastic on table or bed then get a cup of hot water & dip tortillas individually into water & lay out on center of plastic long way 2x3.
5. Once that is done everything else should be ready to fill the burrito.
6. I would layer beans then the rice in center of the burrito long way then add eggs, jalapenos & cheese.
7. Last but not least, add the hot chips or any chips you choose really Doritos, Chili Corn chips, etc. You can also add pork rinds if you prefer but it makes it a little harder to roll.
8. Once everything is portioned on the center of the tortilla long ways it is time to roll – literally.
9. The first thing you want to do is fold in the ends about 1-2" after that use the plastic to roll the burrito slowly for a perfect arm length burrito make sure you keep the ends in & roll until the burrito forms. Once it is rolled in plastic twist ends & tie.
10. Then push the ends in to compact the burrito & make an arm length breakfast burrito
11. Poke a couple holes in the plastic.
12. Then cook in microwave until hot & serve… Enjoy!

Candied Oatmeal

Ingredients:

Regular Oatmeal Packet
Oreo Cookies
Plain M&Ms

Directions:

1. Make Packet of Oatmeal Per Instructions.
2. Mix in Crumbled Oreos &/or Plain M&Ms.

*If you like a little more chocolatey taste add the M&Ms as you're making the Oatmeal.

Breakfast Cakes

Ingredients:

4 Breakfast Cakes
4oz Peanut Butter
3oz Syrup
6oz Oatmeal Cookie
1 Banana
½ Box of Raisins
½ Cup Milk
2 Bowls

Directions:

1. Break down Cakes.
2. Chop up banana & mix with cake in bowl.
3. Pour syrup in bowl & mix.
4. Break down cookies to dust.
5. Add cookies to bowl mix.
6. Add milk & stir.
7. Separately add peanut butter & syrup together in separate bowl.
8. Take cake out of bowl.
9. Spread peanut butter & syrup on top of cakes & enjoy!

Time to Shine

Every action has a reaction
So think before you move
The game of life is chess not checkers
Find your ambition and thrive
Strategical power moves
To stay out them shower shoes
Keep your awareness up and stay on your toes
That other shit just that other shit
Focus on goals
These are words of wisdom that I preach
Learn to practice what you preach
At the same time keep an eye on who you teach
These words are to uplift your spirit
I hope they give you hope
Deep breath in deep breath out
I know you have doubt
Put them out of your mind and grind
Baby boy it's time to shine…
It's time to shine!

Honey Bun Delight

Ingredients:

1 Honey Bun
1 Pack of Peanut Butter
1 Packet Peanut Butter M&Ms

Directions:

1. Spread Peanut Butter over Honey Bun.
2. Add M&Ms.
3. Enjoy!

Sweet Popcorn

Ingredients:

Microwave Popcorn
Reeses Pieces
Chocolate Kisses

Directions:

1. Pop Popcorn.
2. Drop Chocolate Kisses &/or Reeses Pieces in Popcorn Bag.
3. Shake Popcorn Bag Real Well.
4. Snack Away!

Banana Pudding

Ingredients:

2 Breakfast Cakes
1 to 2 Bananas
2oz Peanut Butter
1 Cereal Bowl

Directions:

1. Break up cakes very fine to like dust.
2. Slice bananas very thin into bowl & smash together very well, fold & smash & stir.
3. Then add peanut butter & repeat, smash, fold & stir.
4. Once mixed together well – Enjoy!

That's it – really easy & real tasty.

Caramel Apple Lollipops

Ingredients:

2 Green Apple Jolly Ranchers
1 Caramel Cube
1 Plastic Spork (break off spork part)
1 Pill Bottle

Directions:

1. Place 2 Green Apple Jolly Ranchers in pill bottle & melt in microwave.
2. Cut Caramel cube in 4 pieces & place in pill bottle with melted Jolly Ranchers.
3. Place the handle of the spork into the bottle & let sit for 4 to 5 minutes.
4. Then squeeze the bottle until candy loosens & pull out… Enjoy!

Banana Cream Chocolate Cake

Ingredients:

2 Bananas
16oz Bag Chocolate Chip Cookies
1 Milky Way Bar
4 Hershey Chocolate Bars
6 Breakfast Cakes
2 Peanut M&Ms Regular Size
2 Butterfinger Regular Size
5 – 2oz Peanut Butter Packets
6oz Milk
4 – 24oz Bowls

Directions:

1. Crush cookies & cake together in bag or big bowl until it turns to "pie crust".
2. Pack "pie crust" in bowls to make layer all around bowl.
3. Microwave for 30 seconds.
4. Layer inside of bowl (pie crust) with peanut butter.
5. Dice up bananas & pack bowl.
6. Place back in microwave for 45 seconds on high, take out & immediately remove from bowl & let sit for an hour.

Frosting:

1. Take Hershey bars & Milky Way – break up into small pieces in bowl.
2. Add 10 spoons of milk.
3. Then microwave until melted.
4. Let sit for 5 minutes then ice cake.

Toppings:

Crush Butter Fingers or Peanut M&Ms & top cake.

Lollipops

Ingredients:

1 Packet of Jolly Ranchers
1 Packet Lemon Drops
1 Packet Lemon Chewy
1 Packet Gummy Worms
1 Packet Caramel Cubes
8 Plastic Spoons or Sporks (twist off the spoon or spork part)
2 to 4 Plastic Pill Bottles

Directions:

1. Think of different combinations of Jolly Ranchers you enjoy.
2. Place 2 flavors in the pill container & microwave for 8 seconds until melted.
3. Then add whatever candy you prefer: Lemon Drop, Lemon Chewy, Gummy Worm or Caramel Cube (I recommend cutting up).
4. Then add spoon handle to pill bottle & let sit for 4 to 5 minutes.
5. Last, squeeze pill bottle to pop out Lollipop… Enjoy!

Chocolate Covered Honey Buns w/Reese's

Ingredients:

1 Honey Bun
1 Hershey Chocolate Bar
2 Reeses Peanut Butter Cups
1 Bowl

Directions:

1. Break up chocolate bar in a bowl.
2. Microwave 30 seconds at a time until smooth (stir occasionally).
3. Let chill 60 seconds.
4. Pour chocolate over Honey Bun.
5. Break up Reeses into pieces.
6. Put Reeses on top of Honey Bun.
7. Enjoy!

Chocolate Covered Twinkies

Ingredients:

2 Packs of Twinkies (total 4)
1 Hershey Chocolate bar
1 Bowl

Directions:

1. Break Hershey bar into individual squares.
2. Add to bowl & microwave for 30 seconds at a time until melted & smooth.
3. Take out & let chill for 60 seconds.
4. Then pour over twinkies.
5. Let cool a little & then enjoy!

Banana Crumble Cake Pudding

Ingredients:

3 Crumb Cakes
1 Bag Vanilla Cream Cookies
1.5 Bananas

Directions:

1. Place crumb cake in bag
2. Scrape out vanilla cream from the cookies & put into bag.
3. Put 1 banana into bag with cakes & cream filling.
4. Smash in bag & mix together well.
5. Take some cookies & line bottom of bowl.
6. Put hole in bag & squeeze half to layer cookies.
7. Then put more cookies on top.
8. Squeeze another layer of mix on top of cookies.
9. Slice up ½ banana & place on top of pie/
10. Break up rest of cookies & sprinkle on top.
11. Cover bowl & let sit for 15 minutes.
12. Uncover & enjoy!

Boyca's Chocolate Cake

Ingredients:

4 Hot Cocoas
4 Irish Coffee Creamers
2 Swiss Rolls
1 Rice Crispy Treat
1 – 6oz Chocolate Chip Cookie
2 Honey Buns
1oz Syrup
1 Hershey Chocolate Bar
1 Milky Way Bar
1 M&Ms Peanut Packet
2 Jelly Packets
1 Oreo
4 Breakfast Cakes

Directions:

1. Break up Swiss roll, Honey buns, Milky Way bar, Oreos & breakfast cakes.
2. Add 2 hot cocoas & peanut butter to step one & smash/mix together until makes cake like batter.
3. Layer big bowl with plastic wrap & then place cake mix into bowl to form cake.
4. Flip over onto plate.

5. Put cake in microwave for 60 seconds.
6. Break up Rice Crispy & M&Ms sprinkle on top of cake.
7. Break up Hershey's Chocolate in bowl, add 2 hot cocoas, 4 Irish coffee creamers, 2 jelly packets & syrup. Microwave for approximately 40 seconds.
8. Stir really well – this is your frosting – pour over cake.
9. Let sit for 2 minutes then serve.

Yummy!

Cycles of Life

Common sense is essential
Embrace it and strive for perfection
It will help your mind bear fruit
Knowledge is power appreciate it
Wisdom is like a pot luck of both over time

A combination of all three leads to a virtual lifestyle
Change is a beautiful thing
Against all odds trying to be found
Marinating in a cocoon ready to bloom
From a caterpillar to a butterfly
Cycles of life

Yes I feel the evolution coming
From a boy to a man
Stick to the plan and prosper.

Orange Passion

Makes 4 cups

Ingredients:

32 to 34 Oranges
2 ½ 6oz Kool-Aid
1 Plastic Trash Bag
1 Coffee Bag
1 20oz Coffee Cup
2 to 3 Packets of Sugar

Directions:

(Step 1 Make Kicker)
1. You need to make a kicker out of 4 oranges – squeeze into coffee bag & let sit for 48 to 72 hours until bag starts to blow up.
2. Burp the bag & add a couple table spoons of sugar – seal without air in bag.
3. Repeat for 2 days – strain juice & add ½ cup of orange juice & continue for a total of 8 to 10 days until kicker is well fermented & starts to turn juice into alcohol (make sure every 2 days to drain & add fresh orange juice).
4. Once kicker is made take 20 oranges & peel them, then squeeze into juice.

5. It should come out to 2 – 20oz cups, pour into trash bag & add small handful of pulp from squeezed oranges plus your kicker.
6. Then pour 6oz of Kool-Aid into 20oz cup & add water to top & stir.
7. Then add to bag with orange juice.
8. Repeat one more time with other 6oz Kool-Aid.
9. Mix up bag & then put in trash can to start cooking.
10. Once in trash can add 3 – 20oz cups of hot water in trash can to heat bag (or run under hot water in sink).
11. Put a towel over trash can for 20 minutes.
12. Drain water from trash can & repeat every 6 to 8 hours.
13. Bag should start to blow up so make sure you burp as needed.
14. Once bag stops blowing up the pruno should be complete (usually takes 72 hours).
15. Strain drink from kicker & enjoy!

Remember: If you cook it too long & the batch "Dies" it will taste like vinegar, DO NOT DRINK AT THIS POINT!

Jail House Horchata

Ingredients:

2 Cups White Rice
½ Cup Sugar 1 Cup Milk
10 Fireball Candies
5 Cups Water

Directions:

1. Soak 2 cups of white rice in 5 cups of water for 3 hours then smash rice as fine as possible.
2. Strain rice through hair net.
3. Add ½ cup of sugar & 1 cup milk.
4. Put 10 Fireballs in cup with a little bit of water – cook in microwave until they melt down to syrup like substance.
5. Add the fireball syrup into rice mixture – small amount at a time until it reaches your preferable taste.
6. Enjoy!

Cadillac Coffee

Ingredients:

2 Scoops of Coffee
12oz Hot Water
2 Butterscotch
½ 3 Musketeer Bar

Instructions:

1. Add coffee to water & mix.
2. Break up 2 butterscotch candies & mix in.
3. Mix in ½ of a small 3 Musketeers.
4. There you have a nice & tasty cup of coffee.